Gallery Books
Editor Peter Fallon

16 POSSIBLE GLIMPSES

Marina Carr

16 POSSIBLE GLIMPSES

Gallery Books

16 Possible Glimpses
was first published
simultaneously in paperback
and in a clothbound edition
on the day of its première,
5 October 2011.

The Gallery Press
Loughcrew
Oldcastle
County Meath
Ireland

www.gallerypress.com

ISBN 978 1 85235 521 0 *paperback*
     978 1 85235 522 7 *clothbound*

A CIP catalogue record for this book
is available from the British Library.

for Dermot, William, Daniel,
Rosa and Juliette

Characters

ANTON PAVLOVICH CHEKHOV, writer, doctor
MASHA, his sister, a teacher
YEVGENIA MOROZA, his mother
PAVEL, his father
KOLYA, his brother, a painter
ALEXANDER, called Sasha, his brother, a writer and journalist
SUVORIN, friend, newspaper magnate and writer
LIKA, young woman, an opera singer
OLGA, his wife, an actress
TOLSTOY, writer
KOLYA, young Russian in Badenweiler
BLACK MONK, supernatural figure
DR SCHWORER
OLD MAN
WAITER 1
WAITER 2
SERVANT

Set

The set must encompass a hotel room, a train station, two restaurants, several gardens and interiors.

I suggest a bare space with a table and chairs. A backdrop that spans the length and width of the stage. On this backdrop Russian paintings of the period, magnified. A different painting for each scene. These paintings along with lighting will be paramount in creating the many different atmospheres in the play. (Levitan's paintings are stunning. Also a close friend of Chekhov's. Also look at Chagall and designs for Diaghilev's ballets.)

Music

Also hugely important. From Russian church music to folk to gypsy to piano. All to create mood and tone.

16 Possible Glimpses was first performed in the Peacock by the Abbey Theatre as part of the Dublin Theatre Festival, on Wednesday, 5 October 2011, with the following cast:

ANTON PAVLOVICH CHEKHOV	Patrick O'Kane
MASHA	Catríona Ní Mhurchú
YEVGENIA MOROZA	Bríd Ní Neachtain
PAVEL	Mark Lambert
KOLYA	Gavin Fullam
ALEXANDER	Malcolm Adams
SUVORIN	Michael James Ford
LIKA	Deirdre Mullins
OLGA	Cathy Belton
TOLSTOY	Gary Lilburn
KOLYA	Aaron Monaghan
BLACK MONK DR SCHWORER }	Will Irvine

Director	Wayne Jordan
Set/Costume Designer	Naomi Wilkinson
Lighting Designer	Sinéad McKenna
Audio Visual	Hugh O'Conor
Sound Design/Composer	Sam Jackson
Movement	Sue Mythen
Audio Visual Technician	Patrick Kickham
Design Assistant	Cáit Corkery
Audio Visual Operator	Muireann O'Neill
Set Construction	The Natural Construction Company
Scenic Artist	Vincent Bell
Wigs and Make-up	Val Sherlock

ACT ONE

Scene One

Badenweiler. The balcony of a room in the Hotel Sommer. Darkness.
We hear the laboured breathing of ANTON PAVLOVICH CHEKHOV. *Let*
us listen to this fight for breath a while.

Lights up. We see ANTON *standing in the stifling heat. Quartet*
music from below. A fan whirrs.

Suddenly the BLACK MONK *is there. A tall gaunt figure in black*
robes and cowl. We never see his face. He stands there till ANTON
registers him.

ANTON So you tracked me down?

BLACK MONK What is distance to me, or time for that matter?

ANTON You take unfair advantage. Don't have the energy
to stave you off anymore.

BLACK MONK It's not a war, Anton Pavlovich.

ANTON Believe me, from this vantage point it is. I'm only
forty-four.

BLACK MONK You think eternity cares whether you're nine or
ninety?

ANTON Go away. You don't exist. I must've finally lost it.

BLACK MONK Oh, but I do exist. Don't be afraid. I've watched
you since you were a boy, came out of a thousand
year sleep to watch you live. There isn't a thing
about you I don't know, so don't be afraid.
Eternity has always had its claim on you. Why
should that surprise you?

ANTON Doesn't surprise me. It shames me.

BLACK MONK Why does it shame you?

ANTON I'd have liked more of eternity here.

BLACK MONK And so you're not prepared?

ANTON Give me five more years.

A knock on the door. The BLACK MONK *disappears.*

Come in, it's open.

Enter KOLYA, *a student.*

KOLYA Was wondering if you needed anything.

ANTON Could you pass me that glass of water, please?

KOLYA *does.* ANTON *can barely hold the glass. His hand trembles as he drinks.*

KOLYA You don't want to lie down?

ANTON Better to keep moving.

KOLYA Yes . . . but . . . it's hot, isn't it?

ANTON Unbearable. Isn't there a cooler room?

KOLYA The whole place is a furnace, maybe at the back. I'll ask them again.

ANTON Thank you.

KOLYA Those reporters from home are still in the lobby. They keep asking about you.

ANTON Don't let them near me.

KOLYA Certainly not.

ANTON And don't give them any information about me.

KOLYA God, no.

ANTON You're Moscow, aren't you?

KOLYA Yeah, and you're from the south.

ANTON A lazy southerner. And what brings you to Baden-weiler, you don't look sick.

KOLYA No, the brother. My mother sent me to keep him company, only he doesn't want my company. Are you hungry?

ANTON No.

KOLYA Just your wife said to take care of your lunch order.

ANTON You're very kind. Kolya, isn't it?

KOLYA Yeah.

ANTON I had a brother Kolya. He was a painter. A very gifted painter. Could have been better than Levitan.

KOLYA 'Had'?

ANTON Drink . . . women . . . the dreaded bacilli.

KOLYA Oh, I'm sorry.

ANTON Yeah, the same as me . . . For years I wouldn't name my disease, thought to confuse it, thought if I didn't acknowledge it, it would go away . . . I nursed Kolya at the end, carried him from room to room like a child, the wild eyes of him. Then I couldn't watch anymore. I'm waiting for a train and a telegram comes. Three words. KOLYA IS DEAD.

KOLYA Keats nursed his brother too.

ANTON That's right. Tom, wasn't it? The brother?

KOLYA And Keats was a doctor too.

ANTON And Keats was one of God's own.

KOLYA What do you mean?

ANTON He came with it all, just had to transcribe it.

KOLYA Many would say the same about you.

ANTON They're wrong. As usual. Every word, every line has been a struggle for me. Do you have a few minutes to spare?

KOLYA I've all the minutes, nothing to do here.

ANTON Yeah, the women are hogs, have you seen the state of them in the dining room, lashing into the grub, sweat pouring off them — Will you write a letter for me? There's paper there. What date is it?

KOLYA June 30th.

ANTON Okay? Mariya Chekova, Autka, Yalta, Rus. Got that?

KOLYA Yeah.

ANTON Masha, why haven't you written? Where are you? We're still at the Hotel Sommer and will be a while yet as I've had a bit of a setback. I'm high as fifty kites, thanks to the morphine. The food is gorgeous but my ruined stomach can't take it, so I watch Olga eat. The people here have the fattest arses I've ever come across and so satisfied with themselves that I'm glad I don't have to wander the streets looking at them. I miss my garden. How is my new cedar? And how is Mamasha? Is she sparing the ink too? Olga got her teeth fixed and bought me a new suit you could wrap four times round me. The poor fool thinks she's married to a giant. Be well, be happy, be good to the poor, look after my old mother, and don't be alarmed this is not my handwriting. I'll be fine in a few days. Let me sign it.

KOLYA If I run down now I'll catch the post. Need anything from the shops?

ANTON No.

KOLYA I'll be able to tell my grandchildren that I wrote a letter for Chekhov.

Exit KOLYA.

ANTON Long, long ago, once upon a time, the end.

Lights.

Scene Two

Saint Petersburg. Train station. A military band, off. A choir. Noise and bustle from a huge crowd. Trains. Whistles. Smoke. Din. Enter OLGA KNIPPER *in travelling clothes. She powders her face and puts on lipstick as she is followed by an* OLD MAN *wheeling a coffin on a trolley.*

OLD MAN It's light. Is it a child, mam?

OLGA What?

OLD MAN Lost a child myself, mam.

OLGA (*Looking around*) What are you on about?

OLD MAN It's when they hammer the lid on.

OLGA (*Shouts*) Masha! Masha!

OLD MAN The worst.

OLGA Masha, over here!

> MASHA *enters.* OLGA *hugs her dramatically.*

MASHA Oh Olga, Olga, what did you do to him?

OLGA And they've a full military band playing for him. All these people. And the choir. They don't usually have military bands for writers, do they?

MASHA The band is for a general that died in Manchuria. What on earth happened to him? I told you not to take him abroad. You never listen. (*Shouts, off*) That's my mother! Let her through! For God's sake, where's she going now? Let her through!

OLGA None of these people are for Anton? None of them? Just you?

MASHA They're all waiting in Moscow.

OLGA But I wired them! I wired all the newspapers. The damn train. They threw him into a carriage with 'Oysters' written on it at the border. They had him on ice.

MASHA (*Shouts*) Sasha! Here! Over here!

OLGA Don't be surprised if you find fish scales all over the coffin.

Enter ALEXEI SUVORIN *on a walking stick.*

SUVORIN Is this Anton Pavlovich?

OLGA Yes, it is. (*Kisses him*) Alexei. Yes, that's all that's left of him now. And the cork flew out of the champagne as he died.

MASHA You gave him champagne?

OLGA I didn't give it to him.

MASHA Over here! For God's sake, she's deaf as . . . he's not allowed to drink. You know that!

OLGA It was the doctor, some doctor thing, they give champagne to one another at the end. And the cork just flew out of the bottle, and a big black moth flapping at the window and fog slithering into the room.

SUVORIN He was angry with me, don't know what I did on him, think he was just tired of me. I bored him, he was very easily bored, but I loved him like a son. More. (*Strokes the coffin*)

MASHA This is what happens when I'm not around. This is all your fault! Dragging him half way round the world. I hope he didn't suffer.

OLGA Of course he suffered. You think it's easy to die? It's not like on stage when they take their last breath. It's awful. Awful. The panic in his face, minutes going by, thinking it's over and then this terrible sound. How are we going to get out of here?

SUVORIN I wrote to him the other day and didn't post it. Said to myself, I'll give him a dose of his own medicine. Can I be of any assistance?

MASHA We better wait till the General goes.

OLGA Is he being buried today? He should be, the heat, the smell, do you get it?

MASHA What smell . . . what are you . . .

OLGA He has to be buried today. He has to. I'm a wreck. I haven't slept for a week.

MASHA What did he talk about at the end?

OLGA He was raving, muttering about I don't know what, sharks, neckties, the Japanese and at the very last he did call my name. Twice.

MASHA Twice? Did he mention me?

OLGA I don't think he did. Should he have?

MASHA You standing there so smug with your corpse. You're only the handmaiden of death. Don't forget that. You don't own him. You meant nothing to him. You dare bring him home like this and you don't even have the decency to tell me what he said.

OLGA You're just out of control.

MASHA Keep your information. Keep it! You show up here blathering about fish scales and moths. You have a nerve. You're talking about my brother! My brother.

Enter YEVGENIA MOROZA. *She kneels at the coffin. She is followed by* ALEXANDER (Sasha).

YEVGENIA (*Stroking the coffin*) That's three of my children you've taken from me . . . and I dreamt about you the other night. You were eating sunflower seeds, a chubby little fella with no shoes, the way you went round as a boy, always chewing on something.

ALEXANDER Tolstoy sent a telegram.

MASHA *and* OLGA *fight for it.* OLGA *wins.*

He's sick himself or he'd meet the train in Moscow. Let's get out of here. Come on, Mamasha.

SUVORIN If you'll allow me I think I can get us through the paperwork fairly quickly. Come this way.

And they exit with coffin.

MASHA Show me Tolstoy's telegram.

OLGA Later. Later. I'm ready to collapse.

MASHA It belongs with his papers.

OLGA Which means it belongs to you now.

Shoves it at her.

Take it then. You're one of those people, no matter what you take it'll never be enough.

And they are off by now.
Lights.

Scene Three

The garden of a dacha at Lintvariov's Estate outside Moscow. Enter
LIKA, *a beautiful blonde in her early twenties. She smokes, drinks a*
glass of champagne. Piano music, off. Enter ANTON. *Radiant. In the*
prime of his youth and beauty. He comes up behind her. Kisses her.

ANTON And how is my nightingale?

LIKA You're a complete flirt.

ANTON Would life be worth living without it?

LIKA You play us one off the other.

ANTON It's my deprived childhood. Can never get enough
attention from women.

LIKA You love-talk me and then you do the exact same
with every skirt that crosses your path. You want
a finger in all the pies.

ANTON Is that what I want?

LIKA I saw you.

ANTON What?

LIKA Smooching the astronomer, the big owl eyes of
her sucking you in.

ANTON You know it's you I want, sweetheart. What can I
do? I've a big band of lazy siblings to support as
well as the old folks.

LIKA Are you sleeping with her?

ANTON We're not married, are we?

LIKA Are you or aren't you?

ANTON Don't tell me there's a grumpy little housewife
lurking behind those golden curls.

LIKA So it's a crime to want to be your wife?

ANTON We wouldn't last a month. You're going to be an
opera singer. Men will throw roses at your
feet. You think I'd allow that? Believe me, you
wouldn't like me as a husband. Where I come
from a wife is a slave. So, Lika, Lika, sweetheart,
enchantress, let me take off your dress.

Undoing her buttons.

LIKA Here? You must be joking.

ANTON We've never done it outside. It's much better. Everything is better outside. I want to take you up, up into the mountains and . . .

LIKA No. They'll see.

ANTON Do what your doctor tells you.

He starts unbuttoning her, kissing her, making love to her. She holds the glass of champagne, smokes.

Just look at you.

LIKA Men'll say anything in heat.

ANTON Yeah, we will . . . You know the only proof of God's existence?

LIKA Women?

ANTON You could ask me for anything now and it's yours, that's what jackasses men are in the presence of beauty.

LIKA Alright. Marry me.

ANTON First I need to sample the goods. I'm a shop-keeper's son after all.

LIKA You won't marry me and you know it.

ANTON I'll give you a life of misery if that's what you really want.

LIKA You don't have a very high opinion of marriage.

ANTON No, I don't. People marry for the stupidest reasons.

LIKA And what will you marry for?

ANTON For sex, of course.

LIKA Stop, will you, someone might come.

ANTON They're all at the same by the river. Everyone's doing it, Lika, everyone except us.

LIKA They're playing cards in the music room. Suppose I get pregnant.

ANTON Suppose you do.

LIKA I only want to be with you.

ANTON Then be with me.

LIKA And then you'll cast me aside like an old coat.

Enter MASHA.

MASHA There you are. I've been all over. Lika, come and sing for us.

ANTON (*Covering* LIKA) Would you ever get lost, Masha!

MASHA You're a right pair of tarts. I'll have to write to the bishop.

Exit MASHA.

ANTON Another reason I don't need a wife. I have Masha.

LIKA I'm getting the first train out of here in the morning. No more love letters. No more invitations to this harem you keep here. And don't you promise me anything again.

ANTON So serious, Lika.

LIKA Three years you've kept me on a string and behind my back riding half of Moscow.

ANTON Flattered you've such a high opinion of my 'riding' abilities.

LIKA I hope someone breaks your heart soon. (*As she exits*) That's assuming you have one.

ANTON Look at the flounce of that ass. She'll be back!

LIKA (*Calls from offstage*) Not this time. I'm off now to bed the first man I clap eyes on.

ANTON Go ahead, who's stopping you? (*Running after her*) Lika, Lika, wait, don't be getting thick over nothing.

LIKA (*Off*) I'm not listening to you anymore, Anton Pavlovich.

And both are off by now.
Lights.

Scene Four

Inside the dacha. Enter KOLYA *in nightshirt, trousers, socks. He is in the middle of a massive haemmorhage, reels and fights for breath.* ALEXANDER *runs on.*

ALEXANDER (*Shouts, off*) Anton! Get in here now! Anton!

> ANTON *enters.*

ANTON Ice. Get some ice and my bag. It's in the hall.

> ALEXANDER *runs off.*

(*Holding* KOLYA) Breathe. That's it. Let it all down, don't stop it, just breathe, don't swallow.

> *Muffled sounds from* KOLYA. *The blood keeps coming.*

Kolya, listen to me. Don't panic. This is nothing. You're going to be fine.

> ALEXANDER *enters and throws bag beside* ANTON.

ALEXANDER There's no ice.
ANTON The fuckin' country's falling down with ice and snow. Get snow! Jesus!

> *Exit* ALEXANDER, *running.*

Kolya, I'm going to give you another shot, okay. Calm now. This'll help. Let's keep it calm. That's it. Good man. That's it.

> *Injects him. Another avalanche of blood.* ALEXANDER *runs on with a fistful of snow.* ANTON *rips* KOLYA's *shirt.*

Pack it on here.

ALEXANDER Is he gone?

ANTON Get more. Go get more.

ALEXANDER *runs off.*

Breathe now. Come on. Come on. It's only a bit of snow.

A terrible breath from KOLYA.

That's more like it. Normally. Don't force them. That's it. The worst is over now. You're alright. I'm here, Sasha's here. You're with us and everything's alright.

KOLYA (*Recovers his breath*) You smell like a hoor.

ANTON You wish.

KOLYA No point washing when there are no women around. What I wouldn't do to a woman right now.

ANTON Goes with the territory, Kolya.

KOLYA What do you mean?

ANTON Oh, when I worked the TB wards as a student the smell of semen'd knock you out, and the women's section — they'd try to pull you into the bed on top of them.

KOLYA I should've been a doctor . . . Never knew dying was such hard work.

ALEXANDER *enters with a bucket of snow.*

ALEXANDER Can I get you anything, Kolya?

KOLYA Vodka.

ANTON Yeah, get him a glass.

KOLYA's *head drops.*

ALEXANDER He's gone. He's gone.

ANTON He's just passed out . . . Have them disinfect the floors. Now. And his sheets changed.

ALEXANDER Is this the end?

ANTON   Surprised he's still with us. Look at his hand, like tissue. I'm out of here this evening.

ALEXANDER   But he'll want you with him.

ANTON   Masha's coming.

ALEXANDER   And if he dies while you're away?

ANTON   I've been nursing him ten weeks round the clock. Where were you?

ALEXANDER   I was working.

ANTON   Drinking your head off more like.

> *And exit* ALEXANDER. ANTON *sits there holding* KOLYA.

KOLYA   (*Waking*) These are not my socks.

ANTON   They're mine.

KOLYA   I'd take the shirt off your back.

ANTON   You would. You have.

KOLYA   I'm keeping you from your writing.

ANTON   I'm a doctor first.

KOLYA   So you keep saying.

ANTON   I only write for money. Whereas you, you're the genuine article.

KOLYA   No. No finishing power. That's the hallmark of the artist. Finishing power. Get it done. Get it done. Onto the next. It's only a sprint against time because nothing turns out as you've truly imagined it. Couldn't be bothered finally, sooner fuck and drink red wine.

ANTON   Wouldn't we all?

KOLYA   You either live or watch other people live. That's the choice. You can't do both. I chose to live.

ANTON   To the hilt.

KOLYA   You think I wasted my life?

ANTON   I think you could've been a little more faithful to what you were given. You know how many artists in this world? Real artists?

KOLYA   None.

ANTON   Almost none. Maybe one in every two million. If even. So when I say you are an artist I'm telling you you were born like that, with the gift, and no one can take it from you except yourself. The battle with others pales in comparison with the battle we wage against ourselves.

KOLYA I've always thought the only thing to do is surrender, surrender with grace. We're shadows, shadows on someone else's path, parasites on the soul, like ticks in a haycock. We know nothing.

ANTON A bit esoteric for me.

KOLYA You think we're all dust.

ANTON I've dissected a few corpses in my time and even the most hardened spiritualist must sooner or later ask himself, where exactly is the soul located?

KOLYA Sweet words to sing me to my rest.

ANTON Yeah . . . well . . .

KOLYA Don't worry, the auld fella'll be in flinging incense and ikons at me in a minute. Where's Sasha gone with the vodka?

ANTON Come on, we'll get you back to bed . . . Can you walk?

KOLYA Let's see.

A painful struggle. ANTON *half-carries him off.*

And what is it about Masha?

ANTON What about her?

KOLYA She hangs on your every word.

ANTON Does she?

KOLYA You ask too much of her.

ANTON I ask too much of everyone.

And they're off by now.
Lights.

Scene Five

A restaurant in Saint Petersburg. Sound of violin. Bustle of people eating, laughing, talking in Russian. Enter two WAITERS. *They set a table. Enter* SUVORIN. *He takes off his coat. Hat. Gloves. Hands them to the* WAITER. *Looks around.*

SUVORIN This the best you can do?

WAITER We're overbooked, sir.

SUVORIN (*Nods to someone*) This place is gone to the dogs. Next I'll be dining with nurses. Vodka. Blini. Caviar.

WAITER Yes, sir.

Enter ANTON *in an immaculate suit.*

SUVORIN Well, if it isn't the escaped convict.

Kisses him, hugs him.

I've missed you.

ANTON Good to be back in Petersburg. This city is intoxicating if you could get rid of the people.

SUVORIN Wait till I take you to Europe.

ANTON Are you taking me to Europe?

SUVORIN Next month. We're going to see Duse, we're going to La Fenice, we're going to Monte Carlo. We're going to kiss Il Papa. On the lips.

ANTON But I just got back. I'm broke.

SUVORIN When did that ever stop you?

ANTON Beginning to feel like a kept woman.

WAITERS *arrive with food and drink, lay it out, serve them.*

I have to settle down, at least that's what everyone keeps telling me. I have to work, read, I'm a complete ignoramus. Hong Kong was fantastic, fell for a Jap, didn't get out of bed for three days.

Have you ever done it with an oriental?

SUVORIN Have you ever done it with two orientals?

ANTON They're very straightforward, aren't they, almost manly, none of this coyness and simpering you get from Russian women about how you've ruined them just because you've given them their first decent orgasm. Good to see you, Alexei.

He raises his glass. They drink shots of vodka. Eat and drink throughout.

SUVORIN And your cough?

ANTON Gone. No blood for eight months. Everyone should go across Siberia in a horse and cart.

SUVORIN You're crazy. Crazy.

ANTON Yeah, so they're saying in the papers, taking the complete piss out of me. Your hacks are the most vicious. Why do you let them take your friend down like that?

SUVORIN Freedom of opinion.

ANTON Freedom? We don't know the meaning of the word. It's a fuckin' police state we live in. Spies everywhere, censors butchering everything I write.

SUVORIN I protect you from the worst of them.

ANTON Why do they hate me so much? People I've never met, spoken to?

SUVORIN They hate you because you're brilliant.

ANTON Plenty out there good as me. They say the stupidest things. I'm a very simple man, I love lying in a field of new-mown hay, love fishing, being around beautiful women, and they want to kill me over a few little stories and plays.

SUVORIN If it's any consolation they hate me too.

ANTON And so they should. You run the press. You're a powerful man. Me? What am I? My grandfather was a slave who had to buy his own freedom, his wife's, his sons'. He didn't have enough to buy his own daughter back but they threw her in as a bonus so she could do the washing up, I suppose.

SUVORIN Don't you understand that's precisely the reason.

ANTON Because my father was born a serf?

SUVORIN You're a maverick, a peasant who has risen above his station. The ones who hold the reins in this godforsaken hole of a country are all gentry or what passes for gentry. You're an upstart, Anton Pavlovich. Why don't you go back to your hovel and chaw on your turnip? They're afraid of you. God knows what you might write next. They have to keep you down. Use it. Turn it on them. Drive them mad. What do they know about anything? Rotten to the core, snub me all the time. I'm one of the richest men here in Peter. Do they invite me in? I have to fight for a table in a decent restaurant. I'm here most nights and look where they put me? While Count Gaga over there dribbling into his kasha, who hasn't paid a bill since the Napoleonic Wars and won't ever, has the pick of the room. Let him. He'll never understand what it is to be self-made, to be born without privilege, and he'll never, never, know the thrill of wrestling the world to the ground.

ANTON It's disgusting if that's the way it is.

SUVORIN They read you, albeit with malice, trying to catch you out, but they do read you. What more do you want?

ANTON I want it all. Houses, children — I suppose that means a wife, you can't really have children without one. But please God and his holy mother not a wife yet.

SUVORIN What is it with you young men and marriage?

ANTON I'd have to poison her. Waking up with this lump beside you, it's not natural.

SUVORIN Nothing wrong with a wife about the place as long as you don't get too involved.

ANTON Some of us are stupid enough to believe in love.

SUVORIN It's not important.

ANTON Some die for it. Some kill. It is important.

SUVORIN And how is Lika?

ANTON Don't talk to me about that one. She ran off with my friend, my ex-friend.

SUVORIN Who?

ANTON Potapenko.

SUVORIN I thought he was married.

ANTON Well, of course he is, and now the little trollop is pregnant somewhere between Paris and Berlin, writing me the most heartbreaking letters. He doesn't give a damn about her.

SUVORIN Well, he got her on the rebound.

ANTON I never finished with her. I just didn't jump when she said jump. And now I'm expected to leap into the breach and rescue her and unborn child from the whole sorry mess.

SUVORIN And why don't you?

ANTON After what she's done? No way! I'm rid of her now.

SUVORIN But it rankles.

ANTON She's made her bed, as they say. Besides, she wasn't bright enough, and I've a very low tolerance for those without the spark. Anyway what use would I be to a woman? Grigorovich told me I'll be dead by forty. (*Raises his glass*) Well, here's to an early exit.

SUVORIN How dare he say that to you! I don't care if he is Grigorovich.

ANTON He dared. You know why? Because he's lived his whole life as a dare. That gives him the right. The Maestro speaking. He also blessed me. He was the first to tell me I could write, that I wasn't a hack, and at a time when I didn't know who or what I was. You don't forget people like Grigorovich. You pay attention and every silver lining has its cloud. So? Live with it. Besides, it wasn't news, only confirms what I already know. (*Drinks*) Sakhalin was an eye opener.

WAITER Are you ready to order now, sir?

SUVORIN Get us a better table first.

WAITER It'll be a while.

SUVORIN We have time. I'm sick watching the rats waltzing across the borscht and your chef scratching his arse with the teapot. Look at him! Look at him! When I was in prison the biggest stick they could threaten you with was Sakhalin.

ANTON And well they might. I arrived at night, fires all over the island, smoke like great dragons swirling in the wind as if some God had taken off his hat and tossed his hair. It was straight out of Dante or Bosch. Bodies writhing round the fires, lawless, naked, screams from the shadows, girls of nine and ten working the waterfront in slips and lipstick. I disembarked with the convicts, all in chains. Some of them didn't know what it was they had done. One man had his five-year-old son with him, clinging to his father's chains for fear he'd lose him in the swarm . . . I saw a man get ninety lashes. By thirty I ran from the courtyard.

SUVORIN Sights a man should not subject himself to.

ANTON Maybe . . . And because there were more men on the island than women any consignment of women convicts caused huge excitement. They'd line up at the pier to watch them coming off the boats, trying to smarten themselves up a bit so as to appear attractive to the women. And then filing into this barn, the women sitting on their beds, the men looking at them, smiling, trying to catch their eye. And if she smiled back or nodded or just returned the look they asked the guards to go and speak with her. And the women asked questions like, 'Do you have a bed?' 'Is it flax or straw?' 'Do you have a samovar? Plates? Pots, a table, chairs, how many?' And if the men had all of these things or some of them, then the woman would say, 'Will you hit me?' And to watch them, talking in whispers, trying to build a life out of nothing, out of the lash and ignorance and despair, you wouldn't do it to a dog and these are our people. And the men for the most part were courteous, made no distinction between old and young women, just wanted a woman, though when I asked they said they'd prefer a woman who could have children. You'd walk by the huts in the evening and see them holding their infants, playing with them after another day of back-breaking savagery and insults. I went to Sakhalin expecting a chamber of horrors and I found one. But I also found beauty. Didn't expect that. Men, women, children condemned for life and shining out of them the soul's magnificent determination to wrestle from this world more, far more, than it is prepared to yield.

SUVORIN So what are you going to do now?

ANTON Going to ask you for more money.

SUVORIN Against the next few stories?

ANTON Don't feel like a writer these days but, yeah, I suppose.

SUVORIN Come to Europe with me, recharge the batteries.

WAITER We've a table by the window if it's to your liking, sir.

SUVORIN And bloody time too.

ANTON I'll need another advance for that, but I'm there already.

SUVORIN *puts his glass on* WAITER'*s tray. And exit.*

WAITER I'll take that, sir. (*Glass*)

ANTON The clientele here are incredibly rude, aren't they?

WAITER Pigs, sir. The lot of them.

ANTON Yeah. Well, as my old mother says, offer it up. Offer it up.

Puts his glass on WAITER'*s tray. And exit.* WAITERS *clear table and exit.*
 Lights.

Scene Six

Melikhovo. Chekhov's Estate outside Moscow. Enter BLACK MONK. *Takes papers out of Anton's desk. Reads. Enter* ANTON *in fur coat and fur hat. Doctor's bag.*

BLACK MONK   You're writing about me.

ANTON   Trying to.

BLACK MONK   And building three schools?

ANTON   A nightmare. Committee lining their pockets, peasants stealing the timber and brick and not a child within fifty miles who can read. And now we're in the middle of a cholera epidemic. They'll all be dead before there's a school finished.

> *Sits wearily.*

BLACK MONK   You're tired, Anton Pavlovich.

ANTON   I'm very tired.

BLACK MONK   And how is Lika?

ANTON   Her daughter died, so she's devastated obviously.

BLACK MONK   And you?

ANTON   She wasn't mine. Have to keep remembering that.

BLACK MONK   Those distinctions mean nothing in the eternal scheme.

ANTON   Yes, I know, but I can't live in the eternal scheme. I have to live here. I have to do it here . . . And they laughed, booed, hissed my beautiful *Seagull* out of Petersburg.

BLACK MONK   Good. That's good.

ANTON   How on earth could that be good?

BLACK MONK   It'll make you a better writer.

ANTON   I disagree. We need encouragement to flourish, like a plant needs the sun. They're a bloodless, loveless, passionless lot. Don't they drink? Don't they have hearts? Don't they yearn at all? Wouldn't know a decent sentence if it bit their nose off.

BLACK MONK   Then don't write for them anymore. Write for the one in a million. Write for two thousand years from now.

ANTON I'm not that altruistic. Yet.

> *Enter* PAVEL. BLACK MONK *dissolves.* ANTON *sharpens a pencil, then another.* PAVEL *lays tea tray on table. Pours for* ANTON.

I pay the servants good money to do that.

PAVEL Yeah, well, afternoons kill me.

ANTON Could you ask them to keep the noise down, just for a few hours?

PAVEL Crowd of wasters. Apart from you. Where would we be without you?

ANTON We'll be out on the side of the road if I don't get some work done, that's where we'll be.

PAVEL Then work. Work. (*Pulls up a chair. Sits*) I've a bit to do myself. I won't bother you. Farm accounts. The temperature, forgot to record it. (*Notebook*) Was minus eighteen this morning. Minus ten at midday. (*Writing*) We had to bring the bull in. Imagine, we're landowners now. I hope my poor father looks down from time to time, hope he sees if I didn't rise my son did.

ANTON Would you ever stop making the peasants call you 'sir', it's ridiculous.

PAVEL They like it, they feel safer when they know who's boss. I watched my father being smashed in the face by thugs who thought they were better than him. By God they'll call me sir and watch me have my wine in the evening, champagne in summer, piano music, ladies and moguls visiting. All thanks to you, God bless you, let me kiss your hand.

ANTON Papasha, stop, will you.

PAVEL No, listen, listen, I'm your father, I deserve your ear, I deserve your respect, a little of your precious time. Everything went wrong for me. Everything. I had no luck. You got all the luck in this house. But lucky or unlucky I'm your father.

ANTON Have I ever denied it?

PAVEL I'm barely tolerated here. Sasha hates me, Misha and Vanya too, only Masha has a kind word. Is it my fault? I worked as hard as the next. And Kolya to be taken so young, my little son, I miss him every day.

ANTON You were very hard on Kolya, Papasha.

PAVEL What do you mean hard on him? If I was hard it was because I wanted him to get on. It's not easy out there.

ANTON You were brutal to him as a child, to Sasha too.

PAVEL And was I brutal to you in your childhood?

ANTON What childhood are you talking about, Papasha?

PAVEL You're a writer. You make things up. You think too deeply and too long. I won't hold it against you but please don't confuse me with your stories about peasants and slaves, the scum of the earth. I'm a good father, just had no luck because you robbed the quota from this family.

ANTON I wish you'd stop lying. For once. I know these things haunt you now. Why not just say, yes, that's the way it was, forgive yourself, try a little tenderness now, a little self-censoring before you speak. It's not too late.

PAVEL But admit it, Antosha, you robbed my place as head of this house when my back was turned.

ANTON Someone had to take charge, Papasha. You ran, left us with nothing. You really think I love you all hanging round my neck?

PAVEL Maybe if you went back to mass, back to your prayers, you might learn a little humanity.

ANTON I don't have time for prayers, I'm too busy feeding all the religious maniacs round here.

PAVEL It's your duty. The young must look after the old.

ANTON And who looks after the young?

PAVEL You're spoiled, soft with privilege. What I wouldn't have done had I your opportunities. You don't know what it feels like when you look at your children and know they're ashamed of you.

ANTON Look, Papasha, I'm not responsible for your un-
happiness, I wish you'd realize that, and really
you must learn to keep your temper to yourself,
do not shout at my mother again under my roof.

PAVEL So now you're telling me how to treat my own
wife?

ANTON I won't have you treat her badly. Not here. Not
anywhere. Those days are gone. Now, please, if I
don't get this finished and in the morning post
there'll be no mortgage paid.

PAVEL Fine, have the last word, you always do. I know
where I'm not wanted.

And exit PAVEL. ANTON *sits there, staring out,
picks up pencil, begins writing. Enter* MASHA.

MASHA Do you have a minute?

ANTON What is it?

MASHA You're working, I'll come back later.

ANTON No, what is it?

MASHA Don't know where to start.

ANTON Start in the middle, trust your listener, don't
invent psychology and always, always cut your
first paragraph, sometimes your last. Cover your
tracks and sing. (*Puts down pencil*)

MASHA Smagin has asked me to marry him.

ANTON And what's that got to do with me?

MASHA You don't think it's a good idea?

ANTON I didn't say that. If you want to marry him, you
marry him, you don't need my approval.

MASHA I'd like it.

ANTON Are you in love with him?

MASHA It's just so sudden, I don't know.

ANTON Marriage is a ludicrous institution. Marriage without is insane. And I don't mean the kind of
love you have for your grandmother. We're talking
white-hot-poker love if there's any chance of it
surviving.

MASHA I'm not saying I'm not in love with him. I mean it
wasn't love at first sight, nothing wild, but he's

grown on me. I could live with him, have children, know I'm not beautiful, but where is it written I can't have my portion like everyone else?

ANTON He'd be lucky to get you, you should have a higher opinion of yourself.

MASHA But what about the old folks?

ANTON What about them? Haven't they a home here?

MASHA I'm afraid it's too much for you, you've taken too much on.

ANTON We'll be fine, I'll probably shoot them in their beds but we'll be fine.

MASHA Just say yes or no. Say no and we'll go on as we always have.

ANTON I can't make a decision like that for you. You must make it.

MASHA But it'd be easier if I said no?

ANTON Well, of course it'd be easier, you practically run the place, but that's not the point. Look, I brought you up, sent you to school, college, so when the time comes you make the big decisions yourself.

MASHA You're a fantastic help, Antosha. What would I do without your advice?

Enter YEVGENIA.

ANTON Maybe it's time to grow up, Masha.

MASHA (*Exiting*) Grow up yourself!

ANTON (*To* YEVGENIA) What is it now?

YEVGENIA There's an old woman at the back door, some-thing wrong with her neck, she's in agony, poor creature. I know you're not to be disturbed but I couldn't send her away.

ANTON Bring her in. I'm coming.

Gets his bag. Stands there a minute.

(*A whisper*) Lika, Lika, Lika.

Lights down.

ACT TWO

Scene One

A sanatorium in the Urals. Aksyonovo. Enter OLGA *reading a letter.*

OLGA   Masha doesn't invite me to Autka, I notice.

ANTON   Since when do you need Masha's invitation?

OLGA   She's raging. Well, she's every right to be. Why did we have to get married in secret?

ANTON   You wanted a big posh party with our mugs all over the papers.

OLGA   And what's wrong with that?

ANTON   It's vulgar, that's what's wrong with that.

OLGA   It's like we're not married at all. These rituals are important. You won't announce me to the world, you're ashamed of your wife.

ANTON   I just couldn't take the speeches.

OLGA   Or worse. You're afraid of Masha.

ANTON   This has nothing to do with Masha.

OLGA   Then why wasn't she told?

ANTON   No one was told.

OLGA   That's not true, my mother was, my uncles, your brothers. She's afraid I'm going to take her place — well, yes, I am.

ANTON   You're too hard on Masha.

OLGA   Always Masha, Masha, Masha, like having a guard dog in my flat, clocking when I come in, when I go out, where I'll be, who I'm having supper with. I work in the theatre, I'm not a nun.

ANTON   That's for sure.

OLGA   You Chekhovs live in one another's ears. It's not normal.

ANTON   If it's so hard having Masha around tell her to find somewhere else to live.

OLGA Jesus Christ, it's Masha I married.

ANTON You can throw my mother in while you're at it. Anyway it was you wanted this marriage. I was fine and dandy the way we were.

OLGA I thought you wanted children.

ANTON I can't throw them out, they're helpless.

OLGA Thought that was the one good thing about marriage, you get to throw them all out.

ANTON They don't have the cop-on to leave us alone so we must leave them, promise me now.

OLGA (*Sarcastically*) Be nice to Masha.

ANTON Just say nothing and she'll come round.

OLGA Men are great at saying nothing.

ANTON Maybe because you women say too much, like living with a flock of geese.

OLGA And your mother? She'll go mad.

ANTON She won't, she'll pray for you, you'll just be another cross for her to bear in this valley of darkness. (*Wraps himself around her*) Isn't it great we're together though? Aren't you lucky you got such a good catch?

OLGA You're the lucky one! Writers are ten a penny these days.

ANTON Don't I know it.

> *And they're off by now.*
> *Lights.*

Scene Two

Garden at Autka. Enter MASHA *with glass and bottle of vodka.*

YEVGENIA (*Off*) The trees are parched.

MASHA Ah give over babbling for the sake of it. What the hell am I supposed to do here all summer? (*Drinks*) If he'd only come home.

YEVGENIA (*Entering with watering can, gardening gloves*) Let him enjoy his bit of happiness. He works too hard. Everything we have is thanks to him.

MASHA I work too. You think I love teaching those teenage brats? And then I race back to this wilderness to see this house runs, scrubbing, polishing, cooking, weeding, planting, making sure he eats properly. Don't talk to me about happiness. It's for other people. (*Knocking back the vodka*) If he doesn't show up soon I'm going back to Moscow.

YEVGENIA Then go.

MASHA And leave you on your own?

YEVGENIA He'll be back when the weather turns.

MASHA Different ball game now he's tied to that one. She's some operator, sneaking off behind my back like that. Suppose she'll give up the stage now and lord it over us all here, probably throw us out.

YEVGENIA I don't care for her either, but he does, so let him live a little. We won't have him much longer.

MASHA She'll lead him some dance, you wait and see, a tough little madam, that steely German blood, not a drop of Russian in her veins. And she loves the men, a total come-on. Thought he'd have more taste. She doesn't come in till six in the morning, reeking of champagne.

YEVGENIA You like your drink too.

MASHA She sleeps around, she's Danschenko's doll, for God's sake.

YEVGENIA Mariya, she is Anton's wife now.

MASHA Sure she did it here under our very noses. Heard

39

her creeping across the hall.

YEVGENIA Well, maybe you should take less interest in your brother's affairs.

MASHA What do you mean by that?

YEVGENIA If you're not careful you'll turn into one of those hysterical old maids. My family is full of them.

MASHA I don't need to listen to this. I'm going into town.

YEVGENIA In this heat?

MASHA I'm going to send him a telegram. GET BACK HERE RIGHT NOW! He has cut the ground from under me.

Exit Masha. Sound of a bell.

YEVGENIA (*Looks out*) They're burying someone. Of all the places on earth you could build. What does he go and do? He goes and builds beside a graveyard. A Muslim graveyard.

And exit YEVGENIA.
Lights.

Scene Three

Estate near Yalta. Enter TOLSTOY *with newspaper. He stands there reading. Long white beard. Peasant smock. Panama hat. Riding boots. Enter* SERVANT.

SERVANT Your excellency, Chekhov is here.

TOLSTOY Anton Pavlovich. Bring him in. Bring him in.

SERVANT Right away, your excellency.

TOLSTOY If I gave you fifty lashes every time you said 'your excellency' you wouldn't be long changing your tune.

SERVANT But, your excellency, I grew up on Yasnaya Polyana, I've called you your . . .

TOLSTOY Just go, will you, don't keep him waiting.

SERVANT Yes, your excellency.

TOLSTOY You try to raise them up a little, take their snouts out of the trough and they refuse, whole bloody game is impossible.

Enter ANTON.

Anton Pavlovich. (*Kisses him, holds his hands*) This is a treat.

ANTON Maestro.

TOLSTOY Let me look at you. (*Examines him*)

ANTON I'd have come sooner but wanted to let you settle in.

TOLSTOY I'm going out of my mind. Why does anyone bother getting out of bed in Yalta?

ANTON Now we're both exiles.

TOLSTOY You're too thin. You heard I'm sick too? Course you did, front page of the newspapers, all polishing their obituaries, and did you hear I was excommunicated?

ANTON I did. Congratulations.

TOLSTOY Can't be buried in consecrated ground.

ANTON Do you want to be?

TOLSTOY Don't want to be buried at all. Come, sit, we'll

have some tea. (*Rings bell*) Are you hungry?

ANTON Always, but I can keep nothing down, better if I don't try.

TOLSTOY (*Mopping forehead*) This bloody malaria, can't shake it. I want to go home, can't stand the stupidity of the locals and the women are ugly as sin, how can you bear it?

ANTON I've no choice in the matter.

SERVANT *appears.*

TOLSTOY Bring tea. You want anything stronger?

ANTON Tea is fine.

Exit SERVANT.

TOLSTOY Saw your *Three Sisters* before I was carted down here.

ANTON Haven't seen it myself yet, how was it?

TOLSTOY Stick to the stories. You're Pushkin in prose, at times even better than Pushkin, and that's saying something, but your plays, Anton Pavlovich, your plays, I'm sorry, but they're woeful.

ANTON This one is particularly bad, the censor cut it to ribbons.

TOLSTOY Censor aside, where's the drama is what I want to know? Nothing happens, where do your characters take you?

ANTON I've no idea and I care less.

TOLSTOY I'll tell you where, from the sofa to the spare room and back again.

ANTON Isn't that a journey of sorts?

TOLSTOY It may be an odyssey for a mouse but not for a member of the human race.

ANTON Well, God knows, I don't care much for anything I've written, love to burn everything, start from scratch.

TOLSTOY And I saw the Knipper one. She's no beauty and past her first flowering, but a dangerous something in her eye and not a bad actress.

ANTON   We eloped to a sanatorium. For our wedding breakfast we had mare's milk and six raw eggs each.

TOLSTOY   Mr Romance himself.

ANTON   Never thought I'd marry.

TOLSTOY   But you're not really married, are you?

ANTON   What do you mean?

TOLSTOY   Well, she's in Moscow prancing the boards and you're here in Yalta spitting blood. Aren't you jealous?

SERVANT *arrives with tea, serves them.*

ANTON   But if she left the theatre she'd be unbearable, she's a peacock, needs to be admired all the time.

TOLSTOY   They're all the same, there's no peace with them.

ANTON   And my doctors won't let me live in Moscow. I sneak up now and again and she comes here when she can. I know it looks a bit off but I am very married.

TOLSTOY   You're not in love, are you?

ANTON   Wildly, like an Arab. Weren't you in love with your wife?

TOLSTOY   I was, yeah. For about two weeks. After our wedding we took the carriage to Yasnaya Polyana, fucked the whole way home, ate roast chicken and champagne between bouts. When I can't stand her I think of that. I think of that a lot. Did you hoor around much as a young fella?

ANTON   Enough, and you?

TOLSTOY   The biggest tart in Peter and Moscow, I'd have put it in a letterbox. Don't regret it, though I was poxed to the eyeballs at one point, out of action for a couple of years. It's one of the many tenets of our Church Fathers I can't stomach. What are we sparing it for? Look around you, the lord of all creation, the superfluity, the gargantuan excess of the birds and the bees. One glance out the window on a spring morning and you realize the man above was the greatest hoor of all.

ANTON The vagrancy of tulips, the musk of the rose, the come hither of virgin snow. Will I ever see snow again?

TOLSTOY I admire you so much, Anton Pavlovich.

ANTON As I do you.

TOLSTOY There are so many gangsters out there, merchants of literature, cynical, hard nosed, out for gain. You're the only one of the new crop who has a soul. Even when the sentences are terrible, and they often are, but even then, your soul is there, naked on the page. Wish I was so brave.

ANTON You're braver than any of us.

TOLSTOY They're trying to silence me.

ANTON I know and you mustn't let them.

TOLSTOY I'm watched all the time. Followed. Even here.

ANTON They snoop around my house too.

TOLSTOY They leave you with nothing to live for. If you only knew how I clutch at straws . . . Are you afraid of dying?

ANTON Pointless being afraid, ahead of us all. I try not to think about it.

TOLSTOY And how do you do that?

ANTON Keep busy. Work. Work. Work.

TOLSTOY But if you can no longer work?

ANTON Trust your track record. It'll come back, stop fretting.

TOLSTOY I'm telling you, the well is dry.

ANTON And I'm telling you it's just refilling, be patient, you've been writing for nearly fifty years, not even Shakespeare put in fifty years.

TOLSTOY No, something happened after *Karenina*. Don't understand it, but I think when I killed her off, killed some vital part of myself. Whatever alchemy went on in the writing of that book. But I can't put down the pen even though the clear true thing is gone. It's like breathing, Anton Pavlovich, you know that.

ANTON It's like nothing else, but writers are too hard on themselves, on one another. You think the world cares we can no longer express ourselves as eloquently as we once could? Water off a duck, but listen to me now. (*Takes his hand*) People are good because you are alive, they're afraid not to be. You have written beautifully and you will again. Trust me on this.

TOLSTOY Can I read you something I'm trying to hammer out? I've no idea what it's about. Maybe you can tell me?

ANTON Of course, love to hear it, knew you were writing.

TOLSTOY The dog wrote it. It's a complete mess. Have you anything with you? A new story?

ANTON (*Takes manuscript out of his pocket*) I'd like to hear you on this.

TOLSTOY (*Takes it with great interest, weighs it, skims it*) Ten thousand words?

ANTON Bang on.

TOLSTOY And heard you're writing another play.

ANTON Don't believe anything you read in the newspapers.

TOLSTOY I don't. Got this from the horse's mouth.

ANTON Stanislavski?

TOLSTOY What do you make of him?

ANTON He likes to set us one against the other.

TOLSTOY Yeah, wants a play from me too. On what? I said to him, on bloody what? Malaria? Senility? (*Skimming Anton's story*) I used write five thousand words a day.

ANTON Tell me about it. At one point I'd get two stories out a night. And then I'd polish them.

TOLSTOY (*Reading*) A lot of commas.

ANTON Yeah, falling in love with the comma lately.

TOLSTOY Commas are great when you want to move it on quickly. The dash is a full stop plus.

ANTON Yeah.

TOLSTOY (*Reading all the time*) Notice a lot of the younger ones are using the full stop where I'd only use a comma.

ANTON Sentences are definitely getting shorter.

TOLSTOY They are, aren't they? You rarely see the semi-colon now, don't think they know what it's for.

ANTON   Have you come across this recent phenomenon? They're now beginning sentences with 'and' or 'so'.

TOLSTOY That's pure Asia. I haven't come across it. 'And' is good. I'll use that. Where did you see it?

ANTON   Forget, one of those dreadful new writing journals, I think, a couple of gems, the odd half sentence for plunder.

TOLSTOY This is great, no adjectives, clean, clean, clean — that's the ticket, the rest is manna.

ANTON   Manna and maths. None of our esteemed critics have yet figured out that writing is basically mathematics.

TOLSTOY One of us should tell them. How much do you bet they wouldn't believe us?

And they're off by now.
Lights.

Scene Four

Evening. The garden at Autka. MASHA *comes on with glass of wine. Book. Cigarettes. She drinks. Smokes. Reads. Enter* OLGA *in night-dress. Dressing gown.*

OLGA   Do you have a cigarette?

> MASHA *hands her cigarette case. She lights one. Stands there smoking.*

The crickets, just like in *Vanya*. All we need is a guitar.

MASHA   And a gun.

OLGA   You're making it very difficult for me here, Masha.

MASHA   Anton asleep?

OLGA   He's reading Ibsen, keeps slapping his knee and shouting, this man couldn't write 'the cat is on the mat'. He's in ecstasy over Ibsen's faults.

MASHA   You've made a right fool of him now.

OLGA   What?

MASHA   We're not as stupid as you think.

OLGA   Spit it out! Stop torturing me with innuendo.

MASHA   Know damn well what I'm talking about!

OLGA   I've no idea.

MASHA   That baby you lost wasn't Anton's.

OLGA   You're crazy.

MASHA   Am I?

OLGA   This is so twisted. How dare you accuse me like that!

MASHA   Let's talk gynaecology for a minute. I know a couple of things about it. Did a medical course to assist Anton when we had our clinic at Melikhovo. Anton knows a few things about gynaecology too. That was no five-week miscarriage you had. That was an ectopic pregnancy of eight-to-twelve weeks. It couldn't have been Anton's because you weren't here at the time and he wasn't with you in Moscow.

OLGA You're insane.

MASHA Just admit it and I'll leave you alone.

OLGA You're trying to split us up. Does Anton think this too?

MASHA Very hard to know what Anton thinks, know he received a full report from the surgeons who operated on you in Petersburg.

OLGA I've been so sick, nearly died, and now this sneaking around your brother's desk, opening his letters. You're unbelievable, Masha.

MASHA Think you can leave me out in the cold while you swan round in your costumes.

OLGA I? Leave you out in the cold? I live like an un-invited guest in my husband's home, don't go near the kitchen, the cook, the servants, don't open my mouth about the filthy ship you run here. He doesn't eat, doesn't wash, freezes in winter, but you'd rather he died of loneliness here than share him with me in Moscow.

MASHA Suicide for him to be in Moscow in his condition and you know it.

OLGA Lots of consumptives live well in Moscow. The cold hard air is considered better. I've got several opinions on this but you overrule me every time.

MASHA And I'll continue to do so where his health is concerned.

OLGA Just who do you think you are? I include you in my life in every way, a room in my flat, hanging out of me at every gathering, falling around because you can't hold your drink. The Arts Theatre crowd only put up with you because you're my friend, because you're Chekhov's sis-ter, and I'll tell you it's the only reason I put up with you too.

MASHA Well, I won't burden you again or your arty click. I won't interfere with your trysts and liaisons. I'll look after Anton because someone has to.

OLGA You know I love him and would never do any-thing to hurt him. Don't destroy it on us, if not for my sake then for his. Go and find your own man. You're young enough.

MASHA Anton doesn't want me to get married, wants me here for himself. Didn't you know that?

ANTON (*Entering*) That's complete nonsense, Masha.

MASHA Then why wouldn't you let me marry when I wanted to?

ANTON What're you talking about? I never stopped you marrying.

MASHA Well, you never gave it your blessing either. And now you rejig it all to your advantage. Now you have her you haven't a kind word, just orders, orders, do this, do that, hurry, hurry, hurry.

And exit MASHA.

ANTON You scrapping with her again?

OLGA I'm not welcome here.

ANTON Don't be stupid, they wait on you hand and foot.

OLGA Why do you never call a spade a spade? Your mother and Masha hate me.

ANTON Not this again.

OLGA They do. They blame me for losing the baby. My crazy lifestyle. Your mother said it straight to my face. Maybe this marriage is over, never see you anyway, you blame me too.

ANTON Have I said one word? Nursed you round the clock, and I'm meant to be the invalid here.

OLGA Masha said you wrote to Ott and Jakobson.

ANTON Masha should mind her own business.

OLGA That all you're going to say?

ANTON What is there to say? No escaping the surgeon's report. It wasn't mine.

OLGA Then whose was it?

ANTON You tell me.

OLGA You'd trust those surgeons over me. Nearly killed me. Can't believe what you're saying.

ANTON Convince me otherwise.

OLGA What are your brothers saying?

ANTON You don't want to know.

OLGA I absolutely want to know.

ANTON Danschenko. Nemirovich Danschenko, that's what they're saying.

OLGA Do you want us to part?

ANTON (*Looks at her a long time*) Don't know.

OLGA Because I like my glass of wine after a performance I'm accused of lying down with Danschenko?

ANTON Look, I'm here a million miles away, fighting for every breath. You don't write, you don't phone, I don't care whose baby it was only don't lie to me. Let me know who you are whatever the cost.

OLGA It was yours, whatever they say, it was yours. And if you don't believe me I'd rather we split.

ANTON Don't threaten me now.

OLGA I'm not that devious.

ANTON Aren't you? I think I've a fair idea of how it was. You were lonely, I wasn't there, drink on the table, high on your triumphs, the toast of Petersburg, and Danschenko hovering as always. And then your surprise trip here to bed me down. Shhh, don't say anything. (*Kisses her*) I don't care. You're here now, with your husband who adores you. We don't have a lot of time left. I wish I could be better to you.

OLGA Yes, that's how it was. How do you see so clearly?

ANTON Oh, I'm a bit of an expert on human frailty, if nothing else. Besides I've committed every sin against love myself. Now, no more tears. Let's just be good to one another.

OLGA We have to get away from them all, they're killing us, we can't live like this.

ANTON We can. We are. Let's go to bed.

And exit wrapped around each other.
Lights.

Scene Five

Garden at Autka. Enter YEVGENIA.

YEVGENIA Are you gardening in the dark?

ANTON (*Coming on, slowly*) The trees can't stand Yalta either. (*A coughing fit*)

YEVGENIA You should be resting. Is that blood on your hanky?

ANTON One hundred per cent Russian.

YEVGENIA Come in out of the cold. Isn't it enough your father's gone, and Kolya, my poor Kolya, and now you. The Lord above must surely think I need a hammering.

ANTON Leave the Lord out of it, Mamasha, the Lord's world is good, only one bad thing in it. Us. And don't be so quick to bury me. I've put on four pounds since I got back.

YEVGENIA What do I need these leftover years for? If I could give them to you.

ANTON And if I could take them I would. You sure there was no post today?

YEVGENIA I told you.

ANTON Sometimes you forget and I find them in the hot press, under cushions.

YEVGENIA There were no letters, none from Masha, none from Olga.

ANTON Well, you needn't sound so pleased with your news. Why don't they write? Too busy getting plastered. I love to drink too. *The Cherry Orchard* is opening tonight and here we are, Mamasha, might as well be on Mars, could float away right now and no one would care or notice.

YEVGENIA Spring'll soon be here, you can be on your travels again when the thaw comes. Goodnight. (*Kisses him*)

ANTON Night.

YEVGENIA Don't stay out, there's a breeze in from the sea.

And exit YEVGENIA. *Hands in pockets,* ANTON
*stands there. Looks up. Stars. Breeze. Sound of
the sea.*

Enter LIKA.

LIKA Anton.

ANTON Lika. Lika. What are you doing here?

LIKA Trip with my husband. Thought I'd come by to say hello.

ANTON (*Kisses her, holds her*) This is fantastic. You're a life saver. A life saver. Are you well?

LIKA I'm okay. You?

ANTON Never better.

LIKA Olga isn't here?

ANTON You know she isn't.

LIKA Yeah. She's never here, they say.

ANTON Is that what they say?

LIKA They say lots of things. I asked her to drink a toast with me at this party. She refused. A bit of a wagon, all said.

ANTON You think so?

LIKA She has a moustache, Anton.

ANTON I'm trying to get her to grow a beard so we'll look like twins.

LIKA Well, you got what you wanted in the end.

ANTON What was that?

LIKA A part-time wife.

ANTON I never wanted that.

LIKA Didn't you? Can I? (*A drink*)

ANTON (*Pours for her*) Of course, I heard you gave up the opera.

LIKA You heard the opera gave me up. (*Smokes*) I was a disaster. Didn't even make the chorus. You don't know how lucky you are to be gifted. No idea what it's like for the rest of us . . . Why did you shine your light on me so brightly and then just snap it off?

ANTON Never snapped it off. You mistook my dithering for banishment.

LIKA It still goes through me. You loved me, know you did. Don't deny it now.

ANTON I love you still.

LIKA Nothing is right since I lost you. Only went off with Potapenko to make you jealous. I thought to take him from you but I was the one left high and dry. He scurries back to his wife and my daughter dies. Yeah, my baby died at my grandmother's house. Wasn't even there with her. You know why she died?

ANTON It was diphtheria, wasn't it?

LIKA She died because none of us wanted her to live, not Potapenko, not my mother, not you and, terrible though it is to say it, not even me, and so the little creature obliged.

ANTON Our infant mortality rate is a disgrace. You shouldn't blame yourself, Lika.

LIKA I don't blame myself. I blame you. You should've been big enough to take us both on. Don't talk to me about mortality rates. That baby should've been yours.

ANTON Lika, Lika, Lika, don't be like this, it's pointless.

LIKA It's not pointless. Lives are ruined or not ruined and you ruined mine and, in ruining mine, ruined your own. Those weekends in the country. Everyone laughing, singing, shouting, champagne sloshing like there's no tomorrow, you in your summer clothes as loud as anyone. You were so beautiful, so shockingly beautiful. I couldn't take my eyes off you.

ANTON Am I so terrible to look at now?

LIKA (*Hugs him*) Anton, sweetheart, you're dying, aren't you, they're all saying it, I can't bear it and it won't be in my arms.

ANTON I'm not taking it too well myself either. But what can I do, apologize?

LIKA And you wrote *The Seagull* about me?

ANTON Bits of you.

LIKA Come on, Anton, Nina is me.

ANTON Did you mind?

LIKA Got several free dinners on the strength of it. But I sometimes wonder is my life a mess because you wrote *The Seagull* or was it the other way round? Did I follow your plot or you mine? Suppose it doesn't matter now. (*Drinks*) What time is it?

ANTON Stay.

Kisses her.

LIKA You'd be unfaithful to your wife?

ANTON More, I'd be faithful to you for once.

LIKA My husband's waiting at the hotel.

ANTON All these waiting husbands. (*Kissing her over and over*)

LIKA I'm a respectable girl now.

ANTON Not a trait I ever admired much.

LIKA I have to go, Anton.

ANTON Well, don't get too respectable. (*Still kissing her, her hair, throat*) Look at you. How did I ever let you out of my clutches?

LIKA Think of me sometimes.

ANTON I'd walk you to the end of the road if I had the lung power. Be brave, sweetheart. Don't take it lying down. That's all we can do.

She blows him a kiss and is gone. BLACK MONK *stands there as* ANTON *watches her going.*

BLACK MONK Mark her going and mark it well.

ANTON I'm marking it. Was she in the weave?

BLACK MONK Was she in the weave?

ANTON She was the weave . . . Well, goodbye youth, happiness . . . love.

And exit ANTON. *And exit* BLACK MONK. *Lights.*

Scene Six

Gypsy music. A restaurant in Moscow. Enter MAÎTRE D', *followed by* SUVORIN. *A* WAITER *pours wine for him. He reads menu. After a while enter* ANTON. *They embrace.*

SUVORIN So, how's it feel having all of Russia at your feet?

ANTON Hardly all, with ninety per cent of them illiterate and the other ten don't read except maybe reviews.

SUVORIN You're angry with me.

ANTON I am.

SUVORIN Because I let them have a go at you in my paper?

ANTON Look, Alexei, I'm so far from caring what they say about me anymore. I write now what I want to write without ambition or hope.

SUVORIN And you're pissed with me over that big mouth, Zola.

ANTON It would've been so easy to take his side.

SUVORIN Are you out of your mind! They'd have shut me down.

ANTON Would that be so terrible?

> WAITER *comes and pours wine for him. Blini, caviar, etc.*

SUVORIN (*Taking out cigar*) So now my paper's a rag?

ANTON It usen't be.

SUVORIN My paper made you.

ANTON It paid when I needed money.

SUVORIN Think it did more than that. When I met you you were scribbling for every trash magazine in the country. Now you no longer need me, now you can get up on your high horse and preach to me about Zola. What has he to do with anything? A year on Devil's Island'll be the making of him. You're using him to break with me. Fine, but remember this, I made you and my paper made you.

ANTON (*Gets up*) I think this conversation is over.

SUVORIN (*Going after him*) Anton, don't let's part like this. Don't do this to me. I've loved you more than my own sons.

ANTON No one made me, Alexei, no one except myself. I had to draw the slave out drop by painful drop, so don't you ever presume you were remotely involved in my making or unmaking. You flung me a few roubles when I needed them. I gave you back gold every time. It's people like you keep us all beaten down. You did it to Pushkin. You're doing it to Zola. You're trying to do it to Tolstoy. You won't do it to me.

Exiting.

SUVORIN Anton, come on, lighten up for God's sake!

ANTON I've never been part of any faction or gang, don't think a writer can. You're playing dangerous games, Alexei.

SUVORIN What dangerous games?

ANTON Contempt is a dangerous game. Contempt for the truth? The most dangerous, I'd say.

And he's gone.
Lights.

Scene Seven

Garden at Autka. YEVGENIA *sitting, reading her bible. Enter* MASHA *drinking a cup of tea. Followed by* ALEXANDER. *Dishevelled.*

ALEXANDER (*A groan*) Oh God, God, God, where have you hidden the vodka?

MASHA You've drunk us dry, Sasha.

ALEXANDER Where do you keep your stash? My head's exploding.

MASHA Have some tea, it's not even twelve yet.

ALEXANDER And ask the genius for a thousand roubles.

MASHA Ask him yourself.

ALEXANDER I owe a year's rent, these are the only trousers I have.

Enter OLGA.

MASHA You can forget all your schemes, he stays here.

And exit MASHA.

OLGA Good morning to you too.

ANTON (*Entering*) What's up with her?

OLGA She's in a stew because I'm taking you abroad this summer.

ANTON Oh, so you felt the need to tell her already?

OLGA Damn right I did.

MASHA (*Coming back*) I'm not in a stew. You think it's all fun and games. He stays here at Autka and that's the end of it. Anton, you promised.

OLGA Did you?

ANTON The doctors won't let me.

OLGA But you said you'd come to Moscow next month.

MASHA You what?

ANTON And I will. I will.

MASHA You're out of your mind.

ALEXANDER (*To* MASHA) Just one glass.

Exit MASHA.

OLGA No, you won't. She always wins.

And exit OLGA *in a huff.*

ANTON And exit Prima donna in a strop. We don't notice these things here in the sticks.

YEVGENIA Either of you boys realize it's your father's anniversary?

ALEXANDER (*Hungover, standing there*) So?

YEVGENIA So, he was your father.

ALEXANDER Do my best to forget that fact.

ANTON Oh I liked old Pavel at the finish, playing his fiddle in the small hours, polishing his ikons, that puzzled look on his face, something about living he never grasped. We're no better, just trumped up peasants like old Pavel.

ALEXANDER He was a nightmare, destroyed Kolya.

ANTON Kolya destroyed himself.

Enter MASHA *with large glass of vodka for* ALEXANDER.

MASHA That's it, Sasha.

ALEXANDER You're an angel.

MASHA Tell that to your brother, he's acting like I'm his jailer and executioner.

ANTON Sit down, will you, making me dizzy.

MASHA And who'll take the roast out of the oven?

ANTON Sasha will.

YEVGENIA I'll do it.

Exit YEVGENIA.

ANTON Sasha, will you? She burnt herself the other day.

ALEXANDER This should be interesting. Mother and son fight to the death over who takes the roast out of the oven. There's a plot for you. I'll take my usual ten per cent.

And exit ALEXANDER.

MASHA He said last night that there's something wrong with me, that I live too much for you, said I'm sick.

ANTON Sasha's a wreck, never sober now. Ignore him.

MASHA But he's right. I do live for you.

ANTON I want you to know this place is yours when I'm gone.

MASHA That all you have to say about it?

ANTON Also the papers, manuscripts, pretty much everything.

MASHA I don't want your house, your papers, those bloody manuscripts.

ANTON Then what do you want?

MASHA Olga'll go crazy if you leave me this house.

ANTON She won't. You're too hard on her. Try and see her through my eyes.

MASHA You may be in love with her, but Olga's in love with herself.

ANTON You think I don't know that? I'm not in love with anyone. That's the problem. Beware writers who fall out of love. And I'm going abroad with her as soon as the weather turns.

MASHA You can't walk to the end of the garden.

ANTON I've defied the odds this long.

MASHA Have you finished that play yet?

ANTON Why?

MASHA You're a long time at it.

ANTON There's no play.

MASHA What? I thought . . .

ANTON Said everything I want to say. Only subject interests me now is eternity, but I never believed enough in it. And now I find eternity doesn't believe in me.

MASHA If you go you'll come back in a box, but I suppose that's stating the obvious.

    And exit MASHA.
      Lights.

Scene Eight

Badenweiler. Hotel Sommer. ANTON *stands there. Loud and painful breaths. Enter* OLGA *with ice.*

ANTON Can't we move to a cooler room?

OLGA There's a heatwave.

ANTON (*Through terrible breaths*) A room facing north.

OLGA We're in a room facing north. Don't you remember? We moved a few hours ago. Let me open your shirt.

ANTON You don't put ice on an empty stomach. (*Pushes her hand away*)

Enter DR SCHWORER *with the student* KOLYA.

OLGA Thank God you're here.

SCHWORER At least the sun's gone down. (*To* KOLYA) Go quickly and get champagne, the best they have.

Exit KOLYA.

ANTON That bad?

SCHWORER I'm afraid so.

OLGA He can't drink.

SCHWORER It's a doctor thing, we order champagne for one another when . . .

ANTON When it's hopeless.

SCHWORER That's right. Now let's get you comfortable.

ANTON It's easier standing.

SCHWORER Okay.

Silence as ANTON *breathes and breathes.* DR SCHWORER *takes his pulse.*

I ordered your *Collected Stories* today. God knows when I'll have time to read them.

ANTON (*A whisper*) This is it, isn't it?

SCHWORER Yes, it is, my good man, and it's alright. Don't fight for the breaths. They'll come. Slowly, slowly.

That's good. See, they're coming.

ANTON I've done this before . . . many times.

SCHWORER With others? Sure you have, that's it . . . you're
doing fine.

Enter KOLYA *with champagne, glasses.*

Pour for us there, good lad.

OLGA Don't be afraid. I'm here. Give me your hand,
sweetheart.

ANTON Another Russian disgraces himself again.

No sound except ANTON's *breathing. Then a
cork pops.*

What are those scars on your face?

SCHWORER Duelling.

ANTON I thought so. Who was she?

SCHWORER She wasn't worth these, and that's for sure.

ANTON They're very dashing, don't you think, Olga?

OLGA Very romantic.

ANTON When I was a boy all I ever wanted was to fight a
duel like Pushkin, and then to lie on a couch with
my fatal wound, eating cloudberries.

SCHWORER Cloudberries?

ANTON Yeah, he died eating cloudberries. What else would
a poet be eating on his deathbed?

KOLYA *hands around the champagne, three glasses.*
He doesn't drink.

Long time since I had champagne.

SCHWORER Now what'll we drink to?

ANTON I've always hated toasts.

SCHWORER Then we'll drink to silence.

ANTON A man after my own heart.

He drains the glass slowly. Looks out. Hold.
Blackout.